FALLING
THROUGH THE
EARTH

Published by Mac An Leister Press, Inc.
400 Zena Road
Woodstock, NY 12498

Thanks to Gary Irving and Dominick
Amarante for their editorial assistance and
advice. Thanks to Ralph Fletcher, Max
Schwartz, and Sharon Capra Fletcher for
helping make this book a reality.

This book is dedicated to my Mother
and Father.

First Edition, 1991
ISBN 0-9629278-6-4

FALLING
THROUGH THE
EARTH

THOMAS FLETCHER

[signature]

MAC AN LEISTER PRESS
1991

PART I: INTO THE DISTANCE

PART II: BEYOND THE ZENITH

We are falling through the earth,
As all has fallen through the earth,
From somewhere beyond a singularity,
As all is beyond a singularity.
Some time ago, a great explosion,
No greater than an infant's sigh,
Yet bringing with it, time
And all within the reach of space;
And the four great forms of energy,
And the mysterious force that binds them all;
And all matter and anti-matter,
dark and invisible, bound and formless;
Galaxies, gaseous clouds, and interstellar dust,
Quasars, quarks, and black holes,
And all the other strange cosmic animals
And the many types of single stars;
Some dwarf and others giant,
Yet each and every, someone's sun;
And some with planets and others none –
Bright-tailed comets, asteroids and meteors,
And all the other smaller debris
That sail about the solar seas.
And all the myriad forms of planets,
Large and small, cold and molten,
Some with rings and others moons,
Some with life while most are barren…
Yet all with a distinct history,
As all has a distinct history
Read in every atom of its girth.

And there is one which we call Earth,
With an air unlike most others –
Of oxygen, moist and bountiful,
Our windy layer of gold –
Which circles the globe in mighty rivers

And makes the seasonal winds blow,
Up and down, around and around,
Sometimes calm and sometimes bold,
As energies build, release, and expire
In the age-old cycle of moisture.
Then born anew in unfathomable form
As hurricane, squall, or tornado
That spools the wind into merciless frenzies
And drives the rain like cannon fire,
And paints the clouds in shades of corpses,
And splits the sky with tentacles of fire,
And virulent roars that shatter the night.
And there are storms less spectacular,
The common front of day to day,
That makes no special sound nor display,
Except a ballad as it touches the ground
And soaks the land and fills the sea,
And makes the dusty riverbed flow,
And quenches the thirsty pond and swamp,
And makes the gutter vibrate and vomit,
And the meadow sheen in the sun,
And fills the reservoirs that feed the city,
And fills the puddles along the road,
And swells the Great Lakes that elbow each other;
Always falling and somewhere running,
Until it settles to its limits,
As all shall settle to its limits;
Then rising up to fall again,
Appearing then as mist and fog,
Making heavy the hazy day,
Pelting the roof as stones of hail;
Dreamy as drifts of virgin snow,
Prodding the seed to split its shell
And the mountain to melt to silt,

And the forest fire to yield,
And the fungus to rise like spirits;
A constant shower on tropical forests,
Or once upon a desert decade;
Falling on our bright umbrellas
As we make our way across the city.

And so the earth awaits the sky,
Water fingers and fills the land,
Wind sculptures the soil and sand,
Ever changing the countenance of earth.
And the trench is deep as the mountain is high,
And the sky and the sea can be equally blue,
And both can be equally bleak,
And in each can be seen the moon's full brilliance,
And the sea has the whale while land has sequoia,
And both are teeming with life smaller than dust.
And the grasses cling to the dunes and prairie,
Why they appear we can only imagine...

PART I: INTO THE DISTANCE

FIRST BUDS

The first buds
cast a subtle hint
with shy brilliance
upon the Catskill forest.

So wide this veil –
made of bluish red
and yellow bud shells;
poised to deliver
a world of leafy form.

From a distance
it was as if
a great rainbow
lay dreaming in the hills.

ABOVE THE NIGHTTIME KITCHEN DOOR

I read the evening paper,
the hellish details of war,
while a black spider, silent, hung
above the nighttime kitchen door.

The blood within me pounded poison,
thinking of the young men dead;
the spider neither sighed nor shifted,
a stillness cloaked its nest of thread.

Winter thrashed the roof and window,
hurling chairs about the deck,
yet the spider never felt the quiver
that crept upon my stiffened neck.

The paper pictured rows of corpses,
a dark shadow swept the floor,
while a spider hung an eerie portrait
above the nighttime kitchen door.

RETURN OF THE WINTER SKY

Walking in silence
my eyes caught sight
of bright points
and flickering light
through an old sycamore
shifting in the night.

I moved as with a kite
to see what might be,
till a crown of diamonds
appeared above the tree.
Hurried backward further
to the end of the lawn,
found the whole of Orion
and another year gone.

Orion hauling winter along
up above the wakening dawn.
His mighty sword tucked ready,
in trinity star belt neatly aligned,
Betelgeuse robed in radiant red,
a rose amid the thorns of time.

THE WILD FLIGHT

The moon's lean crescent
vaguely illuminated an open field
and black forest outline behind.

Neck tucked, an eerie shriek,
a tall buck,
hiding in the stealthy weeds,
exploded from its knees,
out and upward
in one great scissoring spasm,
pounding field under itself
in furious silence.
A streak of wild earth,
the weight of a large man,
its coat of arms,
tan with white lines,
glowed in the moonlight,
surreal and magnificent.

I spend the days gathering images,
the night in reconstruction,
sowing dreams like patches
along seams of a diminishing world.

THE FIRST WINDS OF AUTUMN

The first winds of autumn
blew one late summer's night;
a cool baritone breeze
gusted with determined ease.

It turned the sky clear and stern,
hushed the insects' wild song,
moths made blankets of their wings,
green leaves shook like bones.

When the wind again grew calm,
the insects made a surge of sound,
as if to mask some great mistake,
as if the time were not so late.

Yet burdened am I,
this life with a mind,
for I know the end is near
long before it will appear.

BENEATH A CORRIDOR OF SUNS

A bright corridor of suns
twisted through the midnight sky,
oozing, soundless, by and by,
above a dark and frozen field.
Some hundred billion stars alight,
drifting through the windless night.

When the east awoke with dawn,
the corridor was lost from view,
then from a sky now vacant blue,
like singing chips of broken night,
a flock of starlings scurried low
across a field of diamond snow.

OUR TIME

The little old graveyard
was never so gay
as when the squall let fall
its load of hailstone
one warm September day.

The birds retreated to the trees,
the wind made streams of colored leaves,
and in the yellow bus that passed
a row of wide-eyed children sat,
their smiles pressed up against the glass,
to view the patch of crooked graves
alive with balls of bouncing hail.

Yet where they sat they couldn't hear,
as down the road they disappeared,
the click of ice against the stone
that made the little graves to groan,
and neither could they dream to know
dancing down the open road
where their names would someday go.

Soon the wind again grew quiet
and the graves fell still as dawn,
and scores of silver stones of hail
vanished in the yellow lawn.

AS THE MOCKINGBIRD SANG

As I raked the leaves,
home on a weekend visit,
I heard my father's voice,
normally subdued,
calling in an unfamiliar way.
A hushed excited yell
rolled across the grass
with the weight of an anvil.
"Quick, come," he said,
"A mockingbird."

I let the rake slip from my hands
and started off across the lawn.
He is calling me, I dreamed,
and I am running to his opened wings,
something the boy within
has longed for all his life.

As his face came clearly into view
I eased my hurried stride,
then stopped abruptly
a careful distance from his side.
His arm already pointed,
upward through a sun-filled sky,
where a sleek gray and brown bird
sat perched upon a rooftop spire.

I craned my neck upward
to view something I'd never seen before,
then listened to its prized recital,
a long medley of intricate sounds;
tweets and hisses, whistles and flutes
pouring magically down from the roof.
With each tune I turned and whispered
to learn in truth from what bird it came.
He answered each with a single reply –
cardinal, catbird, redwing blackbird –
never turning to look in my eyes.

TIME BE GOOD TO ME

You are time,
the great patient one,
the framework from which all is,
from which ships pass point-to-point,
on which the world has come into focus
from the blurred beginnings of eternity.

Time be good to me,
do not let me stray too far,
for I am but a fist of pebbles
sliding toward an angry sea;
I am the moment's confusion
on the face of a stranger;
I am a huge hourglass
stuffed with blood and breath.

Time, for you I wait,
I wait for life to come
outward through these windowed eyes –
for you my precious one.
I wait the winter's cold embrace,
the summer garden's fruitful womb,
the joy of singing flocks in spring,
a field of autumn stars to bloom.
I wait the quick advance of science,
to learn of new historical finds,
and hope they prove opinions right
about things concerning time.

Into the mirror I gaze
to see how time has treated me,
I curse time then
for I see myself already
going back to time,
down the drain and onto the floor,
going back to time,
teeth and hair and youth

sift through time away from me
into pieces smaller than dust.

Yet after time I lust,
and pray be good to me.
Yes, time I say,
before sleep has come:
do not steal me soon,
you the open wound
between past and future
where fate is being made,
the white crest of a breaking sea –
and time is that sea.

Time I beg
be good to me,
although I know
you lend no choices;
you the fruitful road
and the long grave
sprawled about an unpredictable end.
Toward there you point and send me
as gently as the passing day,
like a mother and a madman,
from the orchard to the gangplank,
through love's embrace
to cruel infidelity,
where fragile wings
meet poisonous fangs.

And yet the journey,
this fine odd opportunity,
a brisk walk through Eden,
what can I say?
Only that I wish to see
as far beyond the furthest ridge,
on you that lonesome bridge,
so time be good to me.

BLUER THAN BROWN

Electrons circle an atom's nucleus,
A galaxy whirls in a hurricane of suns,
DNA twists in a double helix,
A cobra coils in a deadly mound.
And the little earth goes round and round
Bluer than brown on a merry-go-round.

A farmer in spring opens a furrow,
The turbine harvests a field of wheat,
Honeysuckle chokes a sapling sycamore,
Young girls hoolahoop on an empty street.
And the dice roll on a sidewalk casino,
And a squall rolls across the sound.
And the little earth goes round and round
Bluer than brown on a merry-go-around.

History turns a familiar face,
The night yields another dawn,
Soldiers return to the trenches
While the bells of a new year toll.
And a man stands to receive his sentence,
And a king kneels to receive his crown,
A newborn infant is raised to the air
While countless die and return to the ground.
And the little earth goes round and round
Bluer than brown on a merry-go-round.

THE PERFECT LAWN

Three serene figures
in white plastic suits
and tight surgical masks
circled slowly about the grass.

The sun was high
in a powder blue sky,
not a bird or a word
nor hum of an insect.

Just a pretty cul-de-sac
in a posh suburban town
and the trickle of toxins
leeching into the ground.

NIGERIAN CHILD

You the edge
of an irrigated field
the flowing waters
do not find.

Your crippled sister
begs along the open sewer.
You laugh and point
when she finds a coin.
Nigerian child,
why do you smile?

Your eyes are pale
yet blossom wide,
as if they hoped to catch
in one inquisitive gaze
a dream so long denied.

Mother sits on earthen floor
quiet, weaving hemp to twine.
She thinks of father toiling
deep within a distant mine.
When she finds you
something small to eat,
you take and dance
around the fire.
Nigerian child,
why do you smile?

Lagos – October, 1983

A HIGHWAY VISION

The highway wandered through
rolling summer fields
with wildflowers ripe and innocent.
Blackbirds flickered red wings,
and a panic stirred in my soul.
The blackbirds seemed to know,
they hung on podded milkweeds
and prodded me to go.

The road came to a place
where dynamite had blasted rock
to neat walls on either side.
Somber bands of ancient sediment,
stark against the living green.
So this the earth, earth –
a bony skull beneath soft hair.
Yet this rock a truer earth,
all life came long afterward,
even the ferns have just arrived.

Then a tide of autumn sunlight
streaming suddenly off the stone
ignited on the open road.
An orange-red metallic glare
caught my senses unprepared.
The rock walls vanished outward
into moonlike vistas of ruin,
and I, gazing from a barren hill,
saw the planet below lifeless and still.

The time of this I could not say,
but my dread-filled heart kept tugging,
and a lone blackbird above me loomed
a presage that the time was soon.

BLACK HOLE

Universe created mind
in its own image.
Mind is a black hole
for matter becoming spirit;
the drawbridge that leads
out of a circle,
into a universe,
to the illusions and truths
of our black holes.

Night prods the mind
to cross the risen bridge.
Closed eyelids stare into black holes,
seek to structure meaning
from the white imaging light
dancing in the blackness.

The universe is a potter's wheel
held in the hands of gravity,
perceived through black holes;
ever drawing our lives to end
as we spin into higher form.

THE INFANT TREE

On the southern shore
of Lake Oneida,
like a crowded cove
of great green sails,
there grew a stand
of ancient trees.
And as the steady
summer breeze
blew the shiny
waxen leaves,
the sound was like
a symphony,
and from a dream
awakened me,
as ocean waves
can call a man.

Breathless beneath
the listing trees,
I lifted eyes
to branches' peaks,
then to the earth
beside my feet,
a tiny stem
and discernible leaf.
And there, behold,
an infant tree,
sown from seed
those above set free.
I silently knelt,
remembering Darwin,
while dreams rode off
toward Galilee.

THE ARTIST WOMAN (For Rosella Hartman)

By age ninety-five
she had left a long wake
of visual dreams.
"Imagine," she once exclaimed,
"if before an artist's death
it all was then lent back to you
for one last review."

Despite a body slight and silvered
her eager eyes still spark with youth,
darting restlessly side to side
like a bluebird snapping off a wire,
as if determined not to miss
a single ray of earthly bliss.

Each day she makes her way
out to the studio
to continue the work
of eighty-odd years.
The talk I heard
as I eavesdropped one June
was not a mind astray
but one utterly consumed.

She had fed the best of nature
into a deep and tireless self.
The mediums mastered,
lithograph and dry point,
water color, oil, and ink,
were the tools used
to immortalize a profound joy,
exotic yet innocent –

that had majestic tigers
peer benignly;
the frozen Woodstock nights
glow in soft mystical light;
young lovers wandering
naked through a Catskill paradise
where mountain and meadow
rise in hues of india ink
that serenade the sky.

She has outlived
sister and brother,
friend and lover,
the sculptor Paul Fiene,
her husband of thirty years.
She has outlived period and passage,
fashion and generation.
She has outlived time.
She holds a water color
completed seventy years before
steady in her dexterous hands.
"I remember," she begins,
delivering a detailed enumeration
of the people, places, and politics
that surrounded its execution.
And then there is a silence,
a time for it to finish echoing
through an ancient well of memory.
A time, a silence, a time.

She walks alone in the woods,
stopping serene and motionless,
as if to take her last
long looks at the world.
She sometimes wakes before the sun
and finds herself crying
but will not say why.
"You just die," she guessed
when asked about heaven,
her raspy voice rising high,
bending in the next breath
to feel the texture
of a stump of rotting birch –
eyes chasing a tiny sparrow
shooting off a sunlit perch.

THE MAN-CHILD

The doctor leaves the room,
she glances from the bed
with eyes dreaming
into the crystal fluid.
An invisible speck of child
she prays will bloom inside.
A marriage of genes
from a donor man
never to be seen.

It will later be born;
the one so long denied.
A birth to fill the ranks
of tired and wounded youth.
A bright lamp of comfort
to burn while turning gray,
and soothe the numb and worry
when nears that final day.

Oh perplexing age –
age of molecular science,
when woman without child
can look from the bed
and glimpse the unborn playing.

See her now, laughing as she runs;
watch him bend for the flower,
dance in new fell snow,
gazing at the moon.

THE EARTHQUAKE

Two opposing
plates of continent
clashed without warning,
renewing a feud
as old as morning.

The earth shuddered,
then heaved forward
with one colossal shock,
maiming the land above for miles
along fractures in the bedrock.

Buildings buckled and peeled,
each an avalanche
of concrete and steel,
crushing like daffodils
the old and innocent,
the princely and the damned,
together in unison,
by the tens of thousands.

And then the fires
leaped upon the nation,
the landscape transformed
into end-time desolation.

And a woman frantic
in the fragments of a school,
and an old man smoking
by a stack of plywood coffins,

and a small boy peering
through a pile of concrete rubble,
and a man flirts with a loaded gun,
and a surgeon severs the mangled limb,
and the nighttime haunted
with the murmuring cries
of a multitude buried alive.

And the land now indifferent,
but a stray tremor;
a curt reminder
that the earth is all things:
the thorn and the petal,
the virus and the pearl,
the maker of continents
and the swallower of worlds.

IN A MOMENT'S HUNGER

I had forgotten
a noonday meal
when, while trimming
the August bluegrass,
there came a bite;
first prod of hunger,
like the empty taut lines
of an orb spider's web.
And as the mind will do,
I sat where I was
and wondered of hunger.

Beyond the field,
beneath the tall pines,
saplings bleed for light
yet there is little –
so they shrivel
like burned children
and die.

Insects stab at my eyes,
far too famished
to consult their instincts.
This is what hunger does.
Like deer in spring
that flock to grassy roadsides,
slaughtered by hurried machines.

And men,
men who strive
so not to be hungry;
they work to live
and work to die

so death has proper ceremony.
Unlike the poor,
born without a prayer,
buried in forgotten fields,
God bless this multitude
who hunger in each.

TWO NIGERIAN KITCHEN KNIVES

On the earthen floor,
the two knives leaned together.

Knives worn from men –
men proud and joyful
with the scent of blood
played about their sleeves;
worn from the friction
of a million calloused hands
swung to clear the jungle;
from slashing thick stems
of plantain and banana,
cassava and yams;
and the umbilical cords
of a hundred infants,
one now sleeping
in the next room.

Together they slashed
a score of whetstones
to black talc.
Both were as familiar
with the throats of mammals
as blind men with braille;
had fought gallantly
side by side
in the Biafran war;
knew the scent of human flesh
and understood why lions
disdain its favor.

They await now the dawn,
jealous of each other's edge,
in a kind of inanimate conspiracy;
a stillness
like the sleeping scorpion
for fools so naive.

THE CHILDREN DREAM OF NUCLEAR WAR

O little ones
small and meek,
to nestled toys
you gently speak,
then curl in stillness
as you sleep.

Tonight you tremble,
twitch with dread,
hot flashes orange-red.
Fire more than sky
(no one to warn)
approaching like
a wicked storm.

You wake with violent shudder,
sweat has wet the bed,
then turns icy cold;
and weren't the grown-ups bold
to hold you with the evening news,
and let you hear while they spoke near.

Try to sleep
O little ones;
pray this nightmare
never comes.
Pray it never really comes.

HILLSIDE DUST

On powdery hill, the edge of Jerusalem,
I stop to think and have a drink,
Eyes notice fragments of tile and pottery,
Kneeling low I gather and sort,
In minutes sweated palms are full,
I have found a blue scarab too.

An Arab boy approaches on mule,
With stick he beats the sad starved face,
Its hooves disturb the hillside dust
Which fountains up the color of rust,
I muster to spit with lips and tongue;
Like smoke it filters to my lungs.

I taste the taste of human soil
And smell the scent of mankind's toil,
Of ages of armies marched into ashes
And flowering cities shaken to crumbs,
Sixty-odd centuries now still as a tomb
Scoffed by wind and scorned with a broom.

THE LITTLE TOWN AND THE WIDE GRAVEYARD

Over the ridge I came,
a bright and faultless day,
to see the houses braced
up along a hillside.

A church spire rose skyward
among the tired black roofs,
its gold crucifix pulsing
through a calm sea of nothing.

On the town's opposing hill,
tall thin engraved stones
spread wide, eye-to-eye –
a panacea for lost souls.

The dead, it seemed,
marching back upon the living,
bigger than a dream,
like ghosts into Armageddon.

THE POD

Through the darkness
the empty milkweed pod
glowed ghostly white.
I plucked it gently
from a bed of black leaves,
slowly moved a thumb
around its sharp rim.
The night was cold and dry,
the wind rose in siren gusts,
the stars frowned downward,
anxious and predatory.

As my thumb continued
round and round the pod's rim,
my eyes keenly followed
a great luminescent arc of stars
a short distance into the universe,
till a wide Catskill shoulder
blinded it from view.

I closed my eyelids,
envisioned the great
galactic arm of stars
looping back upon itself,
winding inward, sleek and tight,
to form a pod of milky light.

THE SPIDER WASP

Your steel-blue wings
sparkled like sapphire
as you fell upon the funneled web
stretched like a demon's bed
along the rickety staircase.

The spider hadn't cause for suspicion.
Summer had been generous,
it had grown obese and cruel,
draining life from an innocent multitude,
then discarding them as dismembered shells
that I swept throughout summer
like rubbish from some glorious picnic.
It had learned to trust its webbed world,
to gauge the meaning of each vibration;
when to remain cautious and alert
and when to rush forward
to harvest its right of birth.

Today the telltale touch was perfect,
the spider lunged to seize its prize,
twice the insect's weight and size,
leaving behind a wake of thread
as it charged across the sunlit web.
Yet when the two faced eye to eye,
the spider lost its urge to kill,
staring instead as if hypnotized
while the wasp remained so strangely still.

Was it a spark of iridescent blue
that singed your eight myopic eyes?
Or some unknown instinctual truth
that remains secret to all but you?
Today those questions mattered little
for the wasp was already upon you,
thrusting a sleek stinger
deep within your fleshy side.
You writhed from a poison
more pernicious than your own,
then quickly sank on eight limp legs,
mortally gored on the carpeted floor
you had mended the night before.

TIDAL STREAM

From bleak decay
marsh grasses rise,
an egret spies
while killie play.

All live and die
to give and receive
in the ebb and flood
of a tidal stream.

MARSH IN FOG

Silent stillness,
thickets of gray.

White columns of steam
twist above a tidal stream.

Flocks of wind
singing unseen.

NEW ENGLAND SPRING MARSH

Garden earth a star-held kite,
returning from a winter's flight,
summons spring to commence once more,
wings veer north above the shore.

Colossal fire on surface sun
(to safely spawn the fin fish run)
reaches marsh as first warm breeze,
snowy ice now liquid steam.

Frozen marsh unveiled and raw,
a great mud corpse all golden straw,
fumes arise unleashed in thaw,
life from death the stringent law.

On elder, young grasses, sly spidery loom,
in salt-poisoned pans sea lavender blooms,
night sky wild returning fowl,
winging, singing, eclipse the moon.

Tidal stream thighs loosen energy,
moon erects estuary, enticing nature's venery,
then ebbs the marsh womb fluid now baptized in decay,
sustains the infant bay life, impending human prey.

Ages on ages of death's debris,
this living bridge between land and sea,
now chimes anew in springtide song,
red-winged blackbird heckles me on.

THE SHALLOW DISTANCE

I looked up at the stars,
roamed eyes in the blackness between,
swept a glance at the Milky Way.

It was late autumn.
Canis Major and Pleiades
blazed little white hot beacons.
They seemed so close –
like lamps from a festive village
across a shallow bay.

Yet I was wishing.
For these were great suns,
stars made tame and dainty
by a distance so unknowable
we can only gaze, dazed –
like snails against aquarium walls.

ON THE FIRST DAY OF AUGUST

There had been spring
and summer rain enough.
The insects and plants
were bursting at the seams,
as if a great single beast
gorged full to torpid sleep.
Yet there was sadness and yearning.

For we were lost
between the fine line
of blossom and snow;
together marching on
to rhythms without rehearsal,
a music cruel and beautiful,
that could not hear our pleas.

EVEN IF THERE WERE

Even if there were
life beyond the soil;
some distant heavenly realm
where spirit is clothes
and nothing grows old.
Gracious would this offer be
yet such a place is not for me.

For I am born of water.
A tiny salty sea
enveloped fetal me
before I emerged
to live as thinking water.
My blood flows
with dark underground streams
to places vile and unclean,
then is born anew in tidal pools
on the ocean's jettied shore.
A measure of pain
rains from my eyes.
I am conceived of water
as the image returned
from the silent spring well.

Of land I know enough,
skull and bone are made of stone.
Hair is desert sand
blown across reachless places.
The brain a rotted log
found deep within the summer bog.
Mountain-peaked aggression

and valley's tender heart;
fertile plains my skin and loins
await the restless plough.
I am a muskrat
trapped in the jaws of a moccasin,
free as arctic tundra
shouldering glaciers.

And of the sky,
I dare not die and leave,
for it is also me.
Raging wild as moment's squall;
confused as sun shower.
The starry night,
my lover's eyes
sparkle, beam and tremble
in vivid midnight ways.
We are Gemini;
together alone.
I am comet
forever coming home,
forever going away.
Youthful as dawn,
fragile as a rainbow's trace,
all lived and understood
in terms of infinite space.

Yes, land and sea and sky
is where I wish to lie
when finally I to stillness go.
The plants and animals,
minute colored spore of fungi,

spotted mushrooms, centipedes,
great sequoia trees
I wish my remains entrusted to.
Let them feast about me,
they are worthy of my flesh.
And when my bones and sinew
go to fragments then to dust
let them swirl above the sea
with the wind freely again.

WHEN I SAY I LOVE YOU

When I say I love you,
it is said with a peaceful tongue
and one lusting blood.
I say it with a depressed soul,
with a spirit indifferent
to the first day of spring,
and one ignited with hope,
like the birth of a star.

When I say I love you
it is said with a mouth of soil
and on my breath
the scent of a salt marsh.
I say it too
with a throat of fire,
with this I hope to blind you,
to use your offered heart
as a podium for my jewels.

When I say I love you
it is meant I wish you banished
forever from my soul.
For I need to be alone,
as only arctic wind could know,
to lick my wounds without your image,
to die without your pity.

When I say I love you
I am begging eternity
to be bonded to your soul,
for you and I together
are like a perfect graft
on some terrible burn.

PART II: BEYOND THE ZENITH

A CONSTELLATION COFFIN

A coffin rose beyond the zenith
slowly through the midnight stars,
drawn behind a tall black stallion,
its scarlet eye the planet Mars.

Four stars framed the ink-night coffin,
three others formed a diamond hinge,
and as it climbed I heard a creaking,
felt my nerves begin to cringe.

I knelt and watched the coffin open
while autumn shiver pierced my skin,
the risen lid revealed a figure
whose only gesture was a grin.

To where might you be going?
Strange the answer he did give,
pointing with a bone-white finger,
yonder toward the place I live.

A coffin rose beyond the zenith,
across the sky it brightly shone,
drawn behind a tall black stallion
riding toward some distant home.

AUTUMN SPIDER

All summer long
I passed you with the slamming door,
hanging on the crooked lamp
when things were hot and damp.
The insects came like shepherd's sheep,
swarmed like city rush-hour streets;
and you, the star of Darwin's rule,
made them look like easy fools,
took advantage of your Spartan tools,
becoming fatter by the day.

At night the streets I roamed,
and as I passed your home
I'd watch you build your web,
transparent sticky threads,
a cunning geometric dread.

One afternoon in mid-July,
I found to my perplexed surprise
that you had caught a tiny toad
and hung it by its brown webbed toes
as hunters hang their meat to bleed.
And funny how you stopped to eye me
while mending lines one break-of-day,
you a seaman perched in lookout
and I the whale you sought to slay?

Toward the end of summer
from two silken pea-sized sacs
your spiderlings had hatched;
tiny grains of amber light,
a thousand, maybe more it seemed,

hung about like infant dreams,
virgin mouths on first spun web
made a golden halo round your head.

One cool September night
I watched you kill a moth in flight;
drawn to dance a lamplight flutter,
caught – my spine an evil shudder.
Its wings were violet-blue,
blending well with twilight hues,
emitting breaths of metallic dust
as they raced to free from hunger's lust.
But tired wings soon lost this pace
enveloped in your clear steel lace.
When hollow body finally fell
one sovereign wing remained to tell
of treasures we may gain in hell.

But Autumn's heart grew cruel;
for weeks you hadn't had a guest,
your web was like a childish sketch,
badly formed and less complex
from frosty wind and tired neglect.
One night we watched the winter stars
climbing mightily in the east,
forcing summer through the past,
an upward flowing hourglass.
So close to death I knew,
I decided then to touch you;
black spiny oil taut back,
finger dreading vile attack,
but as if to show the hope you lacked,
you never even moved.

And I remembered then the time
hiking around Lake Placid
I came upon a wounded doe
kneeling with its head bent low
on a bed of ancient ferns
and black thorned yellow briars.
A gunshot through her back,
a comet trail of blooded track.
I stood about an hour
leaning on a great tall pine,
death about like a choking vine:
she too never moved.

Autumn spider, you the same,
sense the inner life force wane.
You stayed this way one week or so
until the first November snow.
With the dawn I woke and readied,
the downy snowflake, silent, eddied,
and you swaying, wicked, raw,
looking like a falcon's claw,
hung noosed in your own wise fabric
as if for all the villainous deeds –
a fitting outlaw's eulogy.
I cut you down,
black star on virgin snow,
your cradle now the earth below.
And with one tear for living me,
I quietly paused, then let you be.

CITY SHOWER

As I shower above Manhattan
thoughts suddenly ambush –
surprise attack upon myself:
look at your naked body,
strange, evolved creature.

Indefensible panic,
I sprawl about porcelain,
clutch arms to knees,
eyes closed, head between:
pure, this suffering.

THE SKUNK

Sleeping restlessly
within a hot and heavy
Berkshire night.
The air still
as a pool of wax,
and break of day
just moments away.

Awakening.
The high pitched screech
of frightened tires.
A soft crunch,
like hardened snow.
The truck shifting gears
and pushing on into the dawn.

Yet, my lover never moves
while I shake and muse,
until a ghost at last appears,
seeping silent through the screen,
riding an undetectable breeze.
She wakes, gasping for air –
while I imagine chemical warfare.

WINTER MARSH

Warm oozing August mud,
life and death intertwined as one,
has become like frozen rope
waiting as a cobra to spring.

Thorny salt air whipping
starts Spartina singing,
drains the lowland heat,
but ice does keep
a flame beneath,
ready as a cobra to spring.

Marsh below a blanketed snow,
ice-clad tidal flow.
Wetland ecosystem
like Christmas Eve children,
waking at the slightest thaw,
anxious as a cobra to spring.

Winter marsh menopause,
nature told she cannot be.
Silent womb, erected sea,
waiting as a cobra to spring.

HOW WILL WE REMEMBER OUR MOTHERS?

Will it be through childhood's eye,
a love that knows no purer tie;
instinctive bond year long –
and presence like an endless song?
The gods, her gentle temperament
and devils dreaded punishment;
nighttime was her daily death,
the morning dawn her naked flesh.

Will it be as young adults
when finally standing mouth to mouth,
and troubled wings did seek her age
or tides of change had made her strange?
For look we now beyond her cover
as light beyond a midnight sea,
when loins of night eclipse her sphere
like cricket song as winter nears.

Will it be in older ages,
long cleaved apart by life's poor wages;
her colored leaves have turned to snow,
through failing eyes the heartache shows,
then blaze afire like midday sun
when blossoms flare or children come?
Now to the garden she shall go
and soothe with seed what dreams forgo.

THE SHOPPING MALL

I have returned
to a place of childhood,
a place a pasture once stood
and breathed the sun
with a meadow in its heart,
and tall grasses sang
with crickets and chickadees,
and a stream meandered
like a prayer of an ocean,
and wildflowers whispered
like a poem of a forest.

Yes, I have returned
to a place of childhood,
a place where a pasture once stood.

GRAPEVINE ON A SNOWY NIGHT

As the snow sifted
through a black mesh of night
and some ice creaked
on a nearby river,
I knelt, and placed warm hands
on the frozen vine
as thick as my arm.

One hand moved downward
and, meeting earth,
settled in this place of origin.
The other hand moved forward,
toward the sky a little way,
when, at the vine's first division,
it too fell still.

And I now wide apart,
dreamed the heavy fruit,
late summer, swaying full.
Some the birds will eat,
children, those hung low.
The sun shall burst others
and wither what remains,
falling back as dormant seed
to sleep beneath this very scene.

METAL COFFINS

We spend our lives
gorging on the earth,
sucking dry her teats.
Yet when the life,
like a rotted apple,
falls from our flesh,
we have it soaked
in formaldehyde,
dressed in silly
synthetic threads,
enclosed in thick
metal coffins,
airtight, so life
cannot re-enter;
then lowered to the ground,
confusing Mother Earth,
who waits our cold
and stinking corpse
to forge anew.

SONG OF THE NIGHT FIELD

As the last scatter of day
turned to waves of darkening gray,
a great field of night
quickly rose and stood upright,
bared a stark and starry chest
of bright, luminous treasure.

The moon, half-hidden
pondered on the dark hills;
let a gentle light flow outward
upon the living fields of earth.

From the gaping mouth of space
came a glow and a flickering.
The Milky Way bulged downward
through a dark orb of clarity
like a frozen burst of white fire.
Brimming energy without sound,
all tangled in the wondrous ringing
of a grand chorus of insects singing
in long grassy lashes of summer.

I feared it all would damage me
if it had not been so beautiful,
when a voice spoke within and said:
grasp it while you have the mind,
for crickets can not know of rhyme
nor stars of how they brightly shine.
They will sing and twinkle
long past your brief stay.

Yet you are here the only one
who has the means of comprehension;
to sift and choose the world about,
as one might mix a wild bouquet,
then forge it to a moment's wonder,
along this deaf and darkened way.

AFRICAN FIRES

The African fires
ignite into dreams,
dreams to birds and trees,
into villages and laughter,
women feeding newborn,
and hunters killing
in the night forest;

Into a silent man
who tills a small field.
He roasts maize
on scarlet coals,
with a scarred hand
offers an ear;

Into the young woman
who bends near a fire.
She heats water,
bathes a joyful body;

Into a small clay dwelling
covered thick with night,
where a grandmother sings
a soft prelude to infant dreams;

Into the old chiefs
who gather near the fire.
They come to listen,
they come to speak,
each has a long turn
to drain a brimming self.

In the silent dawn
a small girl
goes to the ashes
of last night's flame.
From these coals,
now seemingly dead,
she brings forth fire again.

OF FLOWERS, FILAMENT, AND FLYING THINGS

The flowers bloom wherever they please,
They come and go like spatters of rainbow,
And orchids frown with the beauty of nymphs,
And birds of paradise like the crown of a king,
And roses bleed along the wooden fence,
And a lady slipper sighs beside a spongy bog,
And goldenrod bright as a staff of the sun,
And apple trees in spring with a coat of snowy light.
And the flowers go to peas and pomegranate,
And the flowers go to honey and cider,
And the flowers go to bushels of almonds,
Some are bought to brighten the coffin,
And the groom pins a rose to his black tuxedo,
And one is placed in the barrel of each rifle.
And the flowers go to seed and tomorrow,
For a chosen few shall rise again.
And a burl hitches to the knee of a hiker,
And a sower spaces them along a new furrow,
And wind carries milkweed to a distant pasture;
Some are thrown from a sparrow's intestines,
High in the air twenty miles further,
And some remain where they first fall,
Then return in spring with familiar face
As dandelion or Queen Anne's lace.

And the flowers employ through sweet seduction
What help is needed in reproduction,
And insects enter the bright sweet chambers,
They buzz and hop and crawl and probe,
Stalk and stink and sting and startle,
And fill the air with endless motion,

And katydids ricochet through the August trees,
And hornets hang a perilous paper moon,
And moths coat a street lamp in wool,
And locusts dissolve a field of green corn,
And the gypsy moth turns the forest to webs and ashes,
And a mantis snatches a cricket from its song
While a spotted ladybug plods along
And tsetse flies blacken the lips of a sick child,
And the tarantula hawk surveys the desert for movement,
And the centipede has lived longer than the Tetons,
And the cockroach survived ground zero at Hiroshima.
A tick fastens to the neck of a fawn,
Embeds its mouth like the barb of a fish hook;
By summer's end it is tumid and gray.
An old man studies a swallowtail butterfly,
He holds it gently in arthritic hands.

And spiders are masters of much of this multitude.
And a jumping spider glances sideways at its prey,
And a garden spider hangs a June bug at dawn.
A marbled orb weaver builds its leafy retreat,
It bends the leaf, horn-shaped, as an archer strings a bow;
Beside the retreat it constructs a perfect orb,
Joins a signal wire between the two,
Then patiently waits for someone to ring.
And there are spiders that live in the ground like rodents,
And the trapdoor spider coats its burrow in white silk;
A rustle on top will rouse this fox like a jack-in-the-box.
With leg strokes the fisher spider tickles the pond's surface,
Then drags the stunned minnow up the mossy rock.
And everywhere spiders are snagging and scaling the earth,
And riding the wind on carpets of silk,

Or securing webbed prey with some impossible knot,
Or themselves being pursued by others and caught.

And a hummingbird plucks a yellow crab spider from its
    honeysuckle home,
And a blue jay perches with wolf spider crunched
    within its beak,
And a robin draws an earthworm from its earthen tube,
And a flock of black crows rises above the golden wheat,
A fledgling eagle stares into the canyon abyss,
Like exiled priests, the penguins congregate on the ice field,
The grimy pigeons beg for our melancholy crusts,
A snowy egret spies behind a flange of rushes,
A vulture's head disappears into the ribs of a rotting zebra,
Sea gulls lunge hysterically into the fumes of a trawler,
An angle of geese veers from the tall reactor,
Two cardinals nest in the flowering dogwood.

AMERICAN HARVEST MOON

Strolling past the fourteenth aisle,
one hundred thousand cans complied;
sedate people reaching,
computer checkouts bleeping,
while somewhere high above us loomed
a perfect yellow harvest moon.

THE DENTIST CHAIR

In the small room
all about me loomed
these great machines
obsessed with my teeth.

I wasn't all myself,
aloof without a care –
that sweet inebriating air.
Gazing out a polished window,
a slate-blue Long Island sky,
rising high a perfect steeple,
soothing to the torpid eye.

Oh what wealth can do
for we, the chosen few
who more than survive.

ANDROMEDA

Amid the ancient heros
and immortal stars;
Perseus and Pegasus,
Polaris and Cassiopia,
I had found you.
A pallid burl of light,
like a cotton ball
held against a sea of night.

Standing in the darkness
a man with his dog
stopped to inquire
what it was I saw.
"Andromeda," I replied.

There was a silence.
The dog sniffed my shoes.
I looked about the man's face,
like a black, featureless mask,
then pointed skyward with my arm
at the great spiral galaxy.
Both glanced together upward
then walked away without a word.

We are strangers, I thought,
as I watched them fade.
And when I turned my gaze
to that place beyond the Milky Way,
she, too, had turned away
in a silent cloak of misty haze.

THE TRENCH

A trench resides around me
Forever, night and day,
It follows like a shadow
And will not go away.

It has no space or boundary,
It knows no reasoned code,
It's blind to pain and beauty,
It cares not youth or gold.

This void without reason,
This infinite farewell,
Older than the shape of night,
Younger than a daffodil.

I spend days building fences
To hide its riddle from my senses,
I spend nights with drink and song
To blur its dreadful disposition.

Sometimes I turn and see it
From the corner of my eye,
Waiting in a drift of winter,
Watching in the nighttime sky.

BLUE SKY

You are the tender
beginnings of eternity,
blue sky.

How there could be
tenderness in the infinite,
we can only invent.

Yet the mind searching upward
to cold expanses of space,
first finds you.

And in the early morning
I ask my young love first:
is the sky blue?

WEANED OF HIS FATHER'S KISS

There were woods,
recalled the man,
beyond a stream,
a dark crawl space
in the cellar,
sad June bugs
prying at the screen,
and starlings
joyful in snow.
There were long days
with mother near,
and, when the sun
disappeared,
father would come.
Then darker still,
till day unseen.
Prayers with mother,
kneeling restless.
And last before sleep,
father's kiss.
Not mother's,
soft and warm;
father's kiss was
gentle thorns.

Then one day
he saw a hornet
sleeping on the curtain
but moved too close.
And later that evening,
when lips drew near,

father touched him instead
firmly on the shoulder;
a strange farewell
like autumn chill.
He wept and wondered,
dreamed of thieves,
awoke and worried.

Yet each night after
the same occurred;
he would find the man
and wait before him,
lean forward as a sign,
hold his breath,
plead with eyes.

Never could he ask:
the rain to stop;
a bird to sing.
And never could he dream,
not in a nightmare's nightmare,
the last had come already,
forever come and gone.

With story finished,
he turned away.
His eyes had surged
with hot tears,
yet cooled on his lids
and never fell,
like water
pausing into onyx
on the roof of a cave.

LOVE IN THE AUTUMN SUN

The Catskill forest
rained bronze arrows
of noonday light.
An angelic blue sky
blinked softly
through the tree tops.

A rare autumn air,
warm as rising bread,
drew us to an earthen bed
of new fallen leaves,
bright as the fresh kill.

Yes, God was good,
He was good to the tiger
as sharp mouths attest;
and when her lips
let fall a trickle of blood
I eagerly drank.
Yet, we smiled at this
for wild cats know
the happy scent of blood,
and dagger sharp teeth
to lacerate flesh;
a good and holy sign.

And God blessed birds
with quick keen eyes
to find the hidden prize,
steal from the earth
celebrate to the sky,
as she lifts me
into primordial fire.

He saw it good
to forge great mammals,
beasts who crave sweet things,
will brave a thousand stings,
so claws might clutch the gold.

And trees
with mighty roots
that slowly surge
beneath the loamy soil,
while windblown branches above
crack their huge spines
… quiver, and moan.

IN AN OLD CANNERY IN SYRACUSE

Beneath gray skies
in the outskirts of downtown
looms a great brick structure,
once a meat cannery
in our century's youth.

Standing in its presence,
the wind conjured visions –
countless men and woman
breathed like smoke
into its chambers.
Pride processed along with meat,
enough to make ends meet;
children losing innocent songs
to a symphony of machines.
Oh, those forgotten ghosts
of our American dream.

Yet inside the walls
time has displaced;
artists now fill this space,
quietly pondering lives,
kindling creative fires,
forging visions from metal and clay.

As in the wake
of some terrible fire,
arrives the blueberry bush,
turning ashes to fruit
till new forest takes root.

HEADSTONE

Your garnished gravesite
held solace in contempt.
No keepsake of afterdeath
could summon your smile.

Yet inward you remain,
and there I sometimes find you,
rocking naked in the shadows,
alone and cold as stone.

THE SHUT-IN

She lies on a bed
rolled into yellow folds of mold,
she breathes in a body
exhausted and amputated,
she dreams with a memory
as stark as winter scenery
of a world so long ago,
when words were sung
from the lips of a lover,
and feet walked on windy streets,
and the stars and the moon
were immune to a windowless room.

EAR TO THE EARTH

When I was a boy
my father told me:
"Put your ear to the earth,
and you can hear what is coming
long before it has arrived."

We played this game with vigor.
We heard cars and distant trains;
the thunder and approaching rain.
We imagined things that were not there.

Once he whispered to the earth
with tears and agony in his eyes,
but could not tell me what was said
or if the soil had spoken back.

Tonight I lay in the forest,
a small speck of manhood
eclipsed by a great stand of pines.
My ear upon a loamy bed
and father long since dead.
Yet I can see his tears again
and wonder if the sounds,
those murmured dreams around the bend,
had come before the end.

MOTHER'S COUGH

Sounds of coughing wake me –
choking on the floor below.
I stare into darkness
praying it subsides;
yet it thunders on,
seeping like cyanide
into the room I sleep.

I wrestle from the bed;
move like mink across floor,
then gaze imprisoned
behind banister bars
onto hallway below.

With lifting springs,
she leaves the bed,
afraid it has disturbed
the working man beside.
I glimpse for sacred moment
as she shuts the bathroom door;
fist about mouth, hunching low,
in the dim late hour
looking frail and old.

The sounds of a match
strike and ignite,
conjures in me a dream
of their first night:
beer and perfume in the air,
warm rising smoke
from first cigarettes
tying silver bows
about her hair.

As a young mother,
while he selling far away;
she awake late alone,
sitting by the phone:
a tiny flare of scarlet light
to kiss and tightly hold.

The years until this night,
a sin to someday overcome,
while the world unraveled
and now lies numb.

Tonight the children sleep uneasy,
they taste your blooded throat,
hear the wings of scavenger birds
and pray without words.

SPACE MIGRATION

You sprouted unbridled
from this cruel paradise,
savage and divine.

Now like the inchworm
that reaches the twig's end,
you lift yourself upward
and search the heavens
for a place to take hold.

Ah, humankind,
so cold, so clever,
yet bold beyond measure.

LAST OF THE OCEAN WAVES

We stood beside the rocking sea,
two ocean-hatched New Englanders,
the nephew with his uncle,
a young and older man,
and said nothing for a time.
Watching the waves come from afar;
each swelling into the air,
rising sure-footed tall and stern,
then breaking with a sucking crash,
spilling a rage of white water forward.

He turned to me,
a hand passing confident
through a graying tuft of hair,
and belly hard and overly large
with a long scar purple-red,
"Let's go," he said.

We confronted the sea,
laughing like crazy fools;
he in a boxer's pose
as the first wave rose.
"Dive under," I hollered
before filling my lungs.

We dove in synchrony
into the dark green waist of the waves
as they marched upon us single file.
Sunlit crests swept overhead
then exploded behind our surfacing bodies,
granting just seconds between
to wipe salt from eyes –
gauge the next place of entry.

One wave rose above the others
and threatened to break further out.
I lunged forward to meet it
as it craned its neck upward
in a great cobra hood of fury.

My uncle hesitated and never dove.
The wave knocked him from his feet
then hurled him downward,
in an avalanche of water,
onto the dense ocean floor.
Yet he rose with sufficient time
to stand and face the next impending crest:
a grim wall of silent water
that seemed to drain the ocean into itself.

I dove open-eyed
beneath the closing jaws of the wave.
The ocean floor trembled and shifted
as its huge bulk thundered overhead.
All the while I thought of him,
this tough hero of childhood,
my mother's older brother;
teaching me to throw a punch,
telling stories of the war,
bragging boisterous on the holiday.

My body broke the water's surface
just in time to gaze back
and watch him disappear
in a sand-fumed pool of turbulence.
I hurtled to him

through the grating undertow,
one eye seaward
on the new set of imminent waves.
He reached about my neck,
I dragged him from the churning water,
gray-faced, bleeding from the shoulder,
unable to catch his breath,
with a look of worried sadness
on his cheeks and in his eyes,
as if a flame he thought eternal
had faltered and quickly blown away.

As his furious chest
slowly subsided,
we stood again silent
watching the sea.
Then he took a deep breath
with eyes in the distance
and told in two words
of a voyage's end.
He simply said:
"Never again."

BEACON IN HELL

You really should have listened,
seems there dwelt a premonition
in mother's words that parting night:
"Child use your firelight,
soar wide without fear
and beware the dark corner,
for spiders linger there."

In seconds you were lashed
to the spider's silky rack,
wings wound in liquid steel,
six legs knit to one tight stitch.
Then slowly kissed with lusty fangs,
spewing venom through your veins,
and all the while, as if a curse,
your body boiled, incessantly beamed
a luminous beacon ghostly green.

And to the spider's awed delight
your fire continued glowing bright,
fouled wires within your abdomen
caused light in death to never dim.

The spider patiently put off dinner,
grinning wild at his jeweled prize,
then moved away, silent and sinister,
so other webs could jealously eye.

With the light he washed and groomed
his spiny beard with vile perfumes,
displayed his other dismal wares,

as if he hoped to charge a fare
to view the wings and shriveled thighs
of other careless moths and flies.
Then dozed and dreamed until the day
beneath his lantern on hell's way.

THE LATE SHOW

It is being;
being in time.

I beg the muse
return the wheel
of my illusion.

Questions open
canyon-like,
answers retreat,
never sleep.

AUTUMN MILKWEED

The great weeds rose skyward,
near a wilted field of corn.
Pelican pods grew quickly
like adolescent chests of gold,
seeming ripe by summer's end.

When warm days returned
from a frost-stung September,
the pods split at the seams,
opened wide cotton mouths,
let spill a seeded flurry.

Each spread its silky wings,
flirting with the restless wind,
then lifting, lifting
to the air.
Scores in unison,
as rare as unicorns,
parachuting genes, streaming
out across a vast indifference.

WE MEN WE DIE FOREVER

We men we die forever
From the world eternally severed,
Lost to something less than dust
Turned from flesh to nothingness.

We perish from the land and sea
From pastures green, and tragedy,
We pass away from star and moon,
The night, the dawn, the afternoon.

We go to where no fire burns
We go to where no hope despairs
We go to where no soldier bleeds
We go to where no god shall care.

We fragment down beneath the darkness,
With the wind our ashes soar,
We spread out thin across a wheatfield,
Stripped of life forever more.

Touch me love, the night is cold,
Kiss me love, the warmth consoles,
Take your wings and tightly hold me,
You're going where I cannot go.

We men we die forever,
We flower from a choiceless birth,
We live a life of brave endeavor
Then vanish from the universe.